Training Older Dogs

Miriam Fields-Babineau

CONTENTS

Photo Credits

Photographs by: Miriam Fields-Babineau, Paulette Braun, Isabelle Francais, Alice Pantfoeder, Robert Pearcy, Ron Reagan, Vincent Serbin, Karen J. Taylor, William and Jeanine Taylor, and Shinichi YokoYama.

© T.F.H. Publications, Inc.

Distributed in the UNITED STATES to the Pet Trade by T.F.H. Publications, Inc., 1 TFH Plaza, Neptune City, NJ 07753; on the Internet at www.tfh.com; in CANADA by Rolf C. Hagen Inc., 3225 Sartelon St., Montreal, Quebec H4R 1E8; Pet Trade by H & L Pet Supplies Inc., 27 Kingston Crescent, Kitchener, Ontario N2B 2T6; in ENGLAND by T.F.H. Publications, PO Box 74, Havant PO9 5TT; in AUSTRALIA AND THE SOUTH PACIFIC by T.F.H. (Australia), Pty. Ltd., Box 149, Brookvale 2100 N.S.W., Australia; in NEW ZEALAND by Brooklands Aquarium Ltd., 5 McGiven Drive, New Plymouth, RD1 New Zealand; in SOUTH AFRICA by Rolf C. Hagen S.A. (PTY.) LTD., P.O. Box 201199, Durban North 4016, South Africa; in JAPAN by T.F.H. Publications. Published by T.F.H. Publications, Inc.

MANUFACTURED IN THE
UNITED STATES OF AMERICA
BY T.F.H. PUBLICATIONS, INC.

Training Older Dogs

Miriam Fields-Babineau

This Cocker Spaniel is celebrating her 15th birthday, proving it's never too late to begin training.

After puppyhood most owners assume that their dogs are who they are. However, with training, your dog can become anything you want him to be.

Yes, You Can Teach an Old Dog New Tricks!

HOW DOES AN OLDER DOG THINK?

The attitude of an older dog is similar to that of a person who believes you can't teach an old dog new tricks. The older dog feels he already knows everything and there is nothing that needs changing. In fact, dogs usually reach this knowledge by the age of one year and it is thoroughly set in by two years of age.

They've learned to communicate with others of their species, fought for their place in the hierarchy, know when to eat, where the food is coming from, where their bed is located and when it is time to sleep.

These things were learned mostly through trial and error, often by receiving correction when overstepping the boundaries. Dogs are instinctual creatures, developing an inner sense of timing, place, and behavior.

What we as humans don't understand is that if our pets were left with their parents, they would receive a canine education that would help them fit into their family packs. We have taken them out of their packs and merged them with our own. Without mother dog to teach the pup what is or is not proper, who will? It is now our responsibility.

After going through the difficult puppy stages of housetraining, destruction and high activity, many dog owners feel the job is complete—and if the dog hasn't been given away, its owner has given up in

Before deciding to train an older dog, it is imperative to gain an understanding of how the animal thinks. The better you understand your dog, the more able you will be to apply appropriate training methods.

frustration and allowed the dog full control of the house. The dog tells its owner when to play and eat, that no shoes are safely left outside the closet, and if anything is disagreeable a growl will quickly control the situation.

Some dogs may stop their destructiveness provided they have been confined or otherwise prevented from having access to tasty couches, carpets and new shoes. However, the problems have still not been confronted and solved.

This situation is similar to an adult who never learned to read. The person was able to find work and shelter but was never able to reach intended educational and career goals. In short, the person wasn't guided properly by their parents or simply never had the opportunity. But it's never too late!

How many adult education programs are available to those who wish to finish high school, trade school, or college? Many retirees go back to college to earn degrees that they were simply too busy to accomplish while performing an everyday job and raising a family.

This same situation holds true for dogs. They are never too old to learn. While they may think they know everything and have achieved a high status in your household, they can still learn to become obedient and develop good house manners.

SETTING REALISTIC GOALS

Now that you have made the decision to regain control of the house, you will need to set realistic goals for the relationship between you and your most beloved canine.

One of the most feared myths is that your dog (whom we will refer to as Shadow throughout this book to help personalize him) will stop loving you when you begin asserting your dominance over him. This is totally wrong. All dogs need to have a sense of place and position. They will respect and show more affection to the person who teaches them these things. A dog that knows his position is a relaxed and happy animal.

You will see an entirely new relationship developing as you work with Shadow. It's a relationship unlike anything you have ever experienced with a pet. The two of you become in sync with each other, recognizing moods, communicating, understanding each other's position and needs.

The main fact to keep in mind is that few dogs trained over the age of two years will become show dogs in the

Your dog is never too old to learn, even if he thinks he already knows everything! This fine looking German Shepherd is proof that with time and patience your dog can become a model canine citizen.

obedience ring or otherwise. Most likely your dog was obtained as a companion and pet so you're not worried about this anyway. When setting a goal for the training of your older dog you should keep in mind that perfection may be out of reach and you should strive for simple obedience from your companion and friend. So, even though your Fifi may not become the circus performer you imagined, she can still learn to walk with you without puling you down the street every time she sees a squirrel. And while Shadow may not be able to become a High in Trial obedience champion, he can still learn to come when called so that you don't have to drive around the neighborhood calling out his name hoping that he'll see the car and want to go for a ride badly enough to come to you.

All dogs can learn the basics: heel, sit, lie down, stay and come. Most can learn to perform these basics when surrounded by distractions. Those worked consistently for a long period of time can even learn to listen without a leash when let loose in a quiet area. These are realistic goals.

It is also realistic to teach your dog proper house manners. After all, how many couches and shoes do you need to go through before you simply put the time and effort into teaching your dog that those things aren't a normal part of his diet?

It is up to you to decide when Shadow plays, eats, and goes outdoors to relieve himself. You should never give in to his inciting play by pulling at your clothing, barking, or racing around. It is also possible to allow your house to become non-baby-proofed at some point. Your shoes should be safe if left at the door because they're muddy, and you should be able to pick up a sock or towel when dropped without playing a game of tag throughout the house.

Every dog can learn the terms for proper manners. "Quiet," "Drop-it," "No Bark," "No Sniff" and just plain "No." The word no can have multiple uses for any situation in which the dog is bad, such as jumping up, sniffing the table, begging, mouthing and house soiling indiscretions. It is best to

It is important to set realistic goals when working with an older dog. Perfection is not the goal, a well-behaved and happy dog is.

keep all vocabulary as simple as possible to reduce confusion.

RETRAINING A DOG

You were a responsible puppy owner and took your pup to obedience training when he was young. The two of you went through several months of learning how to sit, down, stay and come. Shadow did pretty well for a while and even stopped chewing the walls and soiling in the house. It was still an advanced aerobic workout when you took him for a walk, but you did train, right?

Shadow just turned two years old and when you came home from work you found the house looking as though it had been hit by an interior hurricane: you know, one that doesn't disturb the outside, just everything that Shadow had access to inside. What happened? The dog knew it was bad to do these things, yet he reverted back to his juvenile delinquent

stage (5-9 months of age) overnight.

Shadow didn't forget his training, he just missed it. When you and he went through obedience school you

A bored dog may become a destructive dog. Training is like an occupation for your pet. Without a meaningful place in your world, he will turn to other means in order to get your attention.

practiced every day for however long your instructor suggested and maintained consistency as much as possible. After a while, Shadow didn't give you any more problems and you stopped working with him.

You may have become extra busy at work or dealing with family matters. Whatever the reason, Shadow found himself with nothing to do with his time. Sure, you'd come home and throw the ball for him, pet him, and see to his feeding and grooming, but the training sessions stopped and so did your best friend occupation.

With nothing better to do, Shadow occupied his time by chewing and digging, a popular doggie pastime. Even though you became angry with him and punished him, at least he got some attention from you, so the behavior continued. Before too long he reverted to puppyhood and no longer respects or listens to you at all.

There is one means of stopping this behavior. Go back into training. Every dog needs an occupation, just as humans do, or they become destructive and apathetic. They need to have something to look forward to each day. They also need a regular

If your older dog was trained as a puppy, but seems to have forgotten all about good behavior, it is time to start retraining. Retraining will occupy your dog's mind, and remind him what's expected of him. He will return to the pleasant companion you once knew in no time.

reassertion of pack hierarchy or they begin to challenge the leader on a regular basis.

The best means of correcting this problem is to restart the training regimen and, if you are still having problems, contact a professional trainer who can accurately address the sources. The source can be as simple as an improper heel, or not coming when called. Sometimes the source can be physical, and a good trainer can recognize this and refer you to your veterinarian.

Sometimes just joining a basic training class can be something that your dog will look forward to doing with you, brining back your harmonious relationship. Shadow will be able to socialize with other dogs, and you will relearn how to give commands and maintain consistency. Remember, dogs don't forget their training, they only miss it.

Joining a training class is a good way to give your dog something to look forward to. Not only will he be engaging in meaningful activity; he will have the opportunity to interact with other dogs as well.

RETRAINING AN ABUSED DOG

Most likely you obtained this dog from a shelter or rescue group. He was given up either because he let someone down due to bad behavior, his owner's situation changed, or he had run away. He was a victim of circumstance and has been separated from those he loved and trusted, if he ever had this situation to begin with. Many dogs are left tied up all day and night without proper food, shelter or socialization. Others are left at the side of the road to fend for themselves. Every one of these situations can be considered abuse.

When you take him home he won't understand your house rules and may jump on the couch or bed simply searching for a comfortable resting area. If he smells food on the counter his first instinct is to reach for it. If he sees water he doesn't care that if isn't in his dish; a puddle or toilet bowl will do just fine. When he sees a strange dog or person who resembles someone who had

When you adopt an abandoned or abused dog, keep in mind that he may never have been exposed to the rules of a home and therefore will not understand what is expected of him.

It is extremely important to continually reassure and praise your dog lavishly during training. You must be patient and consistent without allowing him to run all over you.

hit him, his first instinct is to protect himself by barking aggressively.

Regardless of where Shadow came from or what he experienced in the past, he is still a dog. Canines instinctually have the need for pack order and a consistent environment. Whether the dog is fearful, aggressive, or forlorn he needs guidance to acclimate into his new environment.

This type of dog requires special training. You must be patient and consistent, but this does not mean that you should allow his past to influence your demands. He still needs to learn his place in your family pack, as well as acceptable behavior patterns. He needs to regain confidence and pride in himself. Training him will accomplish these things.

At first he will require more of everything: more good food, grooming, contact, company, bonding activities, solitary walks with you, more exposure to your particular environment, more rides in the car, and more patient training.

Once Shadow begins to regain his health and learns to trust you it is time to consult with a professional trainer. It would be best to begin the training one-on-one, for he may become frightened or overly anxious when confronted with many other people and lunging dogs. The training should be done with coercive methods instead of force methods to teach trust and respect. When he begins to understand simple commands as well as develop confidence in himself, you and the trainer, it's time to join a group or socialization class.

Any dog can be rehabilitated through proper care and training regardless of his past. It will take a lot of work, but the rewards are great. You will have saved a life and formed a relationship unlike any other.

Almost any dog can be rehabilitated after abandonment or abuse. It will take a lot of work and patience, but the rewards will be great and the bond you form unbreakable.

Choosing the Right Trainer

The relationship between you and your dog trainer is very important. It is similar to the relationship that you might have with a therapist. A good trainer will want to know not only about the dog but also about your lifestyle and schedules in order to make certain your pet will learn the appropriate behaviors.

There are several sources to help you find a qualified, certified and highly recommended trainer. The first is the Society of North American Dog Trainers—the first organization to produce both a code of ethics for the training profession as well as a certification test. They can be reached in care of the ASPCA CAS, 441 92nd St., New York, NY 10128.

Another place to search for a qualified trainer is the National Association of Dog Obedience Instructors. They certify their applicants for up to five different levels of expertise. These levels range from beginner to advanced obedience trial and tracking knowledge. They can be reached at 2286 E. Steel Rd., St. Johns, MI 48879.

Before making any decisions find out as much as possible about the trainer. References from your veterinarian as well as speaking to others who have had their dogs trained by that particular person are the best means of getting accurate information.

The most important points to consider about a potential trainer are: Is he/she a humane handler? Does the trainer present the procedures clearly? Is the person patient and tactful, never humiliating or embarrassing towards a student? Are all questions answered and, if not, is the student referred to someone who has the answers? Is the person knowledgeable about your breed?

When you contact the trainer on the phone you can ask him or her about their experience, education, training philosophies and goals, how long the person has been a professional trainer, what will happen when the training is finished (there might be questions or other problems), etc. Ask whether you can observe a training session. You can learn a lot by watching the trainer working with other students. Does the person yell, scream or embarrass the student or is he/she supportive and patient? Is every exercise fully explained verbally and visually? Is the location secure, with little noise so that you can hear the instructor?

—A good trainer will follow a professional code of ethics. The Association of Professional Humane Animal Trainers located in the DC-

Finding the right trainer for your dog is very important. A good trainer will be interested in your pet's lifestyle and tailor his training accordingly.

Be sure to find a qualified, certified, highly recommended trainer for your pet. After all, you will be entrusting your pet's well being to the person you select.

Virginia-Maryland area has devised the following list which all members have sworn to uphold.

—The primary purpose of the group is as an educational body and as such we encourage the sharing of ideas among dog trainers and other animal professionals.

—The idea behind this is that everyone will learn from each other.

—We will promote humane methods of animal training based on sound animal behavioral principles.

—We will maintain the highest professional standards and comply fully with all laws pertaining to the welfare of animals.

—We will promote responsible training, breeding, selling and stewardship of all companion animals.

—We will refrain from public criticism of other members.

—We will not use inhumane treatment, abusive language, or unnecessary force on any animal.

—We will keep an open mind with regard to new training ideas, techniques and equipment.

—We will participate in continuing education activities and share information with other professionals.

—We will practice ethical advertising principles. We consider the unqualified use of the term guaranteed in advertising or promotional efforts to be unethical as there is no sure way to guarantee cooperation and performance of all parties involved, the trainer, the client and the canine student, in addition, implied magical methods or cures are unethical and misleading to the public.

The National Association of Dog Obedience Instructors (NADOI) has a similar list of standards of conduct. They add that "members will endeavor to impart helpful information for the betterment of dog ownership." Also they

Organizations that certify trainers insist that they keep in mind the all-important goals of the dog becoming a willing worker, and being responsible and obedient at all times, not to mention enjoying his training.

make certain the appearance and deportment of members are professional, with appropriate conduct and courtesy. An important point they make is that the instructor should "bear in mind that the problem which brought the owner and dog to them is of primary importance and will direct their efforts to its solution. Solving control problems should not be sacrificed in preference to trial level work."

One of the most important rules of conduct presented by NADOI is that instructors should keep the desired goal in mind of the dog enjoying the training, becoming a willing worker, and above all that he is responsible and obedient with his owner.

Before scheduling a training session, be certain to write down a list of the problems you are experiencing as well as questions, concerns and goals. If you are experiencing an ongoing problem that either hasn't been addressed or in which the methods aren't working, consult your trainer.

While initial consultations with a trainer will vary, there are a few questions that each will ask, normally when you first contact him: the breed, sex and age of your dog, where you got him from, if the dog has been neutered or spayed, his temperament, exercise, health problems, food, the type of behavior problems you are experiencing, and what your goals are. It is best to answer these questions as honestly as you can so that your trainer can devise a system that will coincide with you and your dog.

There are multitudes of benefits to enrolling your dog in group obedience classes. Aside from the training, your dog will socialize with other canines and you will be given a chance to interact with other dog owners.

GROUP LESSONS

These are the most common types of dog obedience lessons available. You can join them through local dog clubs, recreation departments, pet shops, kennels, veterinarians and groomers.

These types of lessons offer the opportunity for your dog to meet other canines and for you to see that Shadow and Fifi aren't the only miscreants in the world. Other dog owners also have to deal with the pulling, chewing, digging, jumping up and excessive barking.

This situation also offers a chance for Shadow to socialize with others. Dogs learn proper socialization skills from other dogs that will be helpful in their development. Also, you will meet other dog owners with similar interests, forming new friendships.

Group lessons are also the least expensive way to train your dog. But inexpensive doesn't always mean quality. While some dogs may do very well in a group environment there are others that do not.

Most group lessons have one instructor and occasionally an assistant or two. There are generally anywhere from 10 to 20 dogs in a group, depending on who is holding the class. The more dogs in the group, the less attention per dog and the better the chance of owner frustration. When many untrained dogs are placed in the same enclosed area the results can be total pandemonium, especially if a few of the dogs are rowdy or aggressive.

A good group class will offer enough instructors and assistants to assure that each student receives proper attention.

During the class the instructor's well-trained dog may be used for demonstration as he/she explains how to perform an exercise. A good instructor will utilize one or two of the student dogs to demonstrate how they learn the exercise, especially if the particular dog chosen is the class clown.

Every instructor will tell you during the first class that success will rely upon your attendance and practice. You are the one being taught, Shadow is the one being trained.

PRIVATE LESSONS

Although more expensive, this is the easiest method of training your dog, provided

Your success in group classes depends greatly on your attendance and the amount of time you spend practicing at home.

you wish to be involved in the process. It is also the best means of addressing specific behavior problems that cannot be covered in a group situation.

Many dogs and their owners don't learn well when confronted with distractions, and this situation will assure that most every concern and training goal is met. Each session is geared to the individual, with every detail taken into consideration and

confronted in a manner that is best for the dog.

Certain dogs that may be aggressive, fearful, or otherwise shy may do better in the private setting. They can learn to overcome their problem behaviors through individual attention and, when ready, join the group situation. Private lessons also offer the opportunity to work with a dog in places where he has specific problems such as his yard, community, a park and in a shopping center.

In-home training more closely mirrors the real-life setting, with Shadow learning to listen where he lives, not just the same enclosed training yard where there aren't any distractions. Would a squirrel dare enter a

Private lessons are often thought of as the best means of training your dog. Having your dog receive individual, personalized training is the best way to train if you have specific behavior problems to address.

Private lessons allow the trainer to come into your home. This allows for the entire family to be included in the training process.

training area where there are 10 or more dogs? Not likely, but he would crawl along the fence in somebody's backyard.

The best thing about one-on-one training sessions is that you can have the trainer come to your home. This not only is more convenient for you—especially if your dog gets car sick—but allows for more flexibility in scheduling.

For a person who is not physically able to keep up with the pace of a group class, this is ideal. This also allows for the inclusion of the entire family. A good private instructor will teach everyone how to communicate and be consistent with the dog. This is especially important with children. While most children under the age of 10 may not be able to do actual hands-on training, they can still learn how to interact with the dog to prevent injuries and misunderstandings.

If the dog has behavior problems such as getting into the garbage, digging, chewing, or house soiling, they are best confronted where they occur. A trainer can "set up" a situation in which the dog will

Even the oldest, smallest and most uncooperative of pet dogs can become a reliable, well-trained canine citizen.

misbehave and then correct the dog while he is in action, thus showing the owner how to perform the correction.

BOARD AND TRAIN

In-kennel training consists of sending your dog away for two to four weeks and having all his training performed by the trainer. When you pick him up he is trained and, hopefully, no longer prone to misbehavior. For the period of time that he is away he is receiving consistent training and behavior modification. This will change his overall behavior patterns, provided it is maintained.

Sending Shadow away is convenient, especially if you are planning on going away for a time. While being boarded your dog will receive constructive attention and learn new things instead of spending his day bored.

If Shadow is difficult to handle and has intimidated you so that you can't walk or reprimand him when he is

Mari, a Golden Retriever, has obviously been well trained by her owners Yumiko Ohori and Shino Bu Mizokami.

bad, then this type of training will be good as an initial behavior modifier with future private lessons once it has concluded. Shadow will return well-behaved, allowing you to learn how to handle him.

While this may be the most convenient means of training Shadow, it tends to be the most expensive and least likely to be successful.

Another thing to take into consideration is the stress on the dog. Anytime your dog leaves his own territory he is stressed, especially if placed in the territory of another dog. In a large kennel with the smells and sounds of many other canines, the stress is immense.

It is also stressful for the dog to be working with someone with whom he is not familiar. It would be a good idea for you and Shadow to meet the trainer who will be working with him during his stay at the kennel.

A very important factor to consider is that you will not be able to observe the training sessions. You will have no idea of the training methods used and whether or not Shadow is receiving proper care, both mentally and physically.

Training your dog yourself will create a strong bond between the two of you that may not be present when someone else trains your pet. Oftentimes a pet will return well trained; however, his owner is unaware of how to communicate with him.

The primary failing of this type of training is that the dog learns but the owner does not, unless the training includes several follow up lessons to teach the owner how to handle the dog. Even with this type of instruction, however, the owner still does not learn how to train, only how to handle. The main difference being that if the dog "tests" his owner by not performing a command properly and is allowed to get away with the minor indiscretion, then he will push the limit further and further each time. For example, the dog is heeling at his owner's side but starts to get a few inches ahead. The owner does not know that his dog is testing authority, and thus the dog is not corrected properly. Eventually the dog will again rule the roost.

It is especially important with this type of training to maintain the work when getting Shadow home again. While many owners may think that their dogs will remain trained even if not practiced with, they are wrong. The reason is not that the dog doesn't remember, it's because his training hasn't been reinforced.

Regardless of the type of training you choose be certain to have full trust and faith in your trainer, as you would a therapist. You are placing a loved one into his care and you need to be able to open your mind to learning without apprehension.

You cannot reach your training goals overnight. It doesn't happen with a magical snap of your fingers. No matter what type of training you choose you will

Whatever means you choose to train your dog be sure you have full trust and faith in your trainer. Your dog is a member of your family and you want him to be treated as such.

need to continue working with Shadow every day for the rest of his life. This takes patience, time and lots of effort.

Your dog needs this time with you. It is his means of working for a living, his occupation. If you slack off and don't work with him, he will revert to misbehaving just to get the attention he once had. We all need something to occupy our minds and look forward to. Shadow needs this, too.

The first thing you must always remember when training your dog is that he wants to please you. Your canine companion will be eager to learn everything you have to teach him!

Teaching Proper House Manners

Your dog should enter [his crate] willingly. Never force [him into] the enclosure, or she w[ill] learn to dislike it.

urinates and defecates [each] time. Do not bring him inside unless he has d[one] both.

6:30 a.m. Feed your [dog.] He can be fed near or i[n his] crate, or somewhere th[at you] can keep an eye on hi[m.]

7 a.m. Take Shadow outside. Again, give th[e] command. Praise and [reward] when he does his deed[s.]

Every 3-4 hours, tak[e] Shadow outside and gi[ve] the potty command. If [he] doesn't potty, put him [in] his crate when your re[turn to] your house. Try again [in a] half hour.

6 p.m. Feed your do[g.]

7 p.m. Take Shadow outside, and repeat eve[ry few] hours until bedtime. D[on't] give Shadow any food [or] treats after this time. T[ake] his water after 8 p.m.

10-11 p.m. Bedtime. [Allow] Shadow to enter his cr[ate] and leave an ice cube i[n his] water dish to keep his [mouth] moist during the night.

HOUSETRAINING

The first part of housetraining is to develop a feeding schedule. A good schedule to stick to is breakfast at 6:30 a.m. and dinner at 6 p.m. The dog's food should be left available for no more than 15 minutes. Whatever is left over can be saved for the next feeding time. This has several purposes. First of all, it teaches your dog to eat immediately, thus reducing a mess if he plays with the food. Secondly, it puts Shadow on a regular diet, maintaining his weight at proper levels. Lastly, and of utmost importance, it allows you to schedule a proper relief time. You will know when Shadow must relieve himself, causing fewer accidents in your house.

The fastest means of housetraining is to crate train him. The crate has many

A good feeding schedule is imperative to housetraining. It will help you to regulate your dog's proper relief time.

uses. It is a place to keep Shadow when you are sleeping or not at home, and it is his very own room to retreat to when he doesn't want to socialize or becomes tired. In short, a crate becomes Shadow's den.

Dogs are natural den dwellers. They like a small space that offers security and where they can feel the sides around them. They will naturally keep their bed clean, relieving themselves outside of their den. This instinctive behavior will aid in your housetraining endeavors.

There are several different types of crates. Metal mesh, that can come in collapsible models, or the hard plastic type that is approved for airline travel. The type you buy should depend upon its usage. If Shadow is not going

One of the fundamentals of good health throughout your dog's life is a sound, healthy diet. Photo courtesy of Nutro Products, Inc.

to be traveling by air t[...] recommend the metal [...] It allows more air flow [...] as greater visibility, ar[...] slide-out tray for easy [...] cleaning.

When purchasing a crate, make certain to buy one that will fit your dog. He should be able to stand to his full height, turn around inside and be able to stretch out.

Crate training should be fun for your dog. He should never have to be forced into the enclosure. In fact, he will go inside willingly if you follow these simple procedures:

—Place Shadow's bed and toys in the crate, and leave it open so that he can investigate it. If he goes inside, praise him and give him a special treat.

—If Shadow is afraid to go inside, place a treat near the opening of the crate, and allow him to take it. Praise him when he sni[...] eventually takes the foo[...]

—When he is no long[...] afraid of approaching th[...] crate, throw a piece of f[...] little further inside.

—Gradually increase

Wh[...]
acc[...]
arou[...]
be a[...]

have to relieve himself more often.

10-11 p.m. Place Shadow in his crate for the night.

If you are abiding by the schedules and procedures I have previously discussed, Shadow should be housetrained within a week.

It is rare for a dog to relieve himself in front of his owners, therefore it is imperative that you keep him with you at all times. Dogs quickly learn your desires and you will need to be very observant of your dog's signals.

Some dogs will whine to let you know of their needs. Others will walk in a circle and sniff. Many, especially those who have been working within a schedule, will walk to the door where they normally go outside.

BEHAVIOR MODIFICATION

All dogs go through different developmental stages throughout their first year. Behavioral studies have suggested that they age 21 "human" years during their first year and five years for each year of age thereafter. This is based on behavioral analysis, not on a physical analysis.

From the age of three to four months, their behavior is similar to that of a six- or seven-year-old child. While still remaining close to their owners, puppies will test to see what they can and cannot do. Many will bite, chew, bark, and try to be bossy. To many new owners these antics appear cute.

From five to eight months, a puppy is an adolescent. At this time they are vying for top position in their pack. They try to intimidate, run off, and

No matter what your schedule, be sure that your dog is allowed ample time outdoors to take care of his needs.

generally act as if they never learned anything. At this age they are also going through some rough teething. Their back teeth are coming in, causing irritability and discomfort. The need to chew is greater than before.

By nine months of age the teeth are all in, but the dog will constantly vie for top position in his pack (your family). If he hasn't learned where his place is, he will be running your household.

The best treatment is

It is important to understand the many stages of life your dog passes through in order to properly assess his training needs.

As a youngster your puppy will age nearly 21 "human" years developmentally in his first year of life. During this time he will challenge his owners to see what he can and cannot get away with.

prevention. Begin the lessons as soon as you get your dog. As a general rule, don't allow Shadow to do anything now that you don't want him to do later—no matter how cute or how much you just want to allow him time to adjust to his new home.

Most likely, if he is still jumping up, chewing, digging, and mouthing, he hasn't been taught not to do these things when he was younger. Each of these has roots in normal puppy play behavior, but will develop into serious problems by the time the dog reaches adulthood. While you are now dealing with an ingrained behavior it is not too late to correct it.

JUMPING UP

Dogs begin jumping up when they figure out that it results in increased attention. It is very clear to them: front legs on a person equals a pat on the head, or a hand to bite on—far more interesting than gnawing on an old bone.

Begin teaching Shadow to not jump by greeting him and initiating play properly. Approach him in a crouched position. This allows you closer contact without Shadow having to reach up for it. It also communicates to him that you desire his attention.

Anytime you are standing still, sitting in a chair, or walking, Shadow should not be jumping on you. If he does, push him down firmly as you say "No!" with a low, growly tone of voice. You should never give Shadow attention because he desires it. The interactions should always be your choice.

This problem will be most prominent when a guest arrives. Not many guests will push your dog away when they are being jumped on. Many will politely say, "It's all right." But they don't mean it.

The cure for this is simple: the No Jump box. This is a device made from a metal container, 15 pennies and an elastic. The metal container can be a soup can, or tea tin— something that's easy to hold in one hand. Place the pennies in the container and wrap the elastic around it so that the pennies don't go flying in every direction on the first shake. It is wise to make several of these, placing them at all doors in the den and in the kitchen.

When Shadow goes to jump up, shake the can hard once

Your dog will do just about anything to gain your attention—jumping up on you is just one way of doing this.

or twice in an up-and-down motion. The sound will startle your dog. If he is startled each time he jumps up he will quickly equate the sound with the action and cease the activity. Do not make any noise with the device when unnecessary; this will cause it to be ineffectual when its need arises.

In the rare situation that you find the sound of the No Jump enhances Shadow's excitement, then you will need to keep him on a leash at all times. When he goes to jump up, tug back firmly on the lead and say No! in a low growly tone of voice.

When Shadow has learned to sit and wait for a greeting, praise him enthusiastically. This is a positive means of reinforcing the proper behavior. Don't get too excited, or he won't be able to control himself. Praise should be happy but not gooey, for some dogs are easily excitable.

CHEWING

Every dog has a need to chew. The trick is making certain Shadow chews on the appropriate things. He should

All dogs like to chew. The trick is providing your dog with appropriate chew toys. Never allow your dog to chew on old shoes or clothes because he will not be able to tell the difference between discarded clothes and new ones.

be provided with a variety of toys. The toys should be rotated daily to provide new stimuli each day.

Large dogs should not be given small objects to play with, such as golf balls, rawhide sticks or chips, or toys meant for small dogs. As a general rule, never give Shadow an old shoe, sock, or towel.

The best toys are those that can withstand rough play, like Nylabones®, which come in a variety of shapes, sizes—even flavors.

Make certain that Shadow has access to his toys at all times. It is also your responsibility to keep an eye on Shadow. Treat him as if he is a toddler. He must remain with you at all times or be confined in an area where he can not get into trouble.

If you catch Shadow chewing on something other than his toys, reprimand him quickly and firmly by grabbing him by the scruff of the neck and saying "No!" in a low growly tone. Place one of his toys in front of him and entice him into playing with it. In this manner you replace the bad thing with a proper

Try to never leave your dog alone for a prolonged period of time. Loneliness leads to anxiety, which in turn will cause problems like chewing and digging.

Dogs require some vegetable matter in their diet. The CARROT BONE™ made by Nylabone®, controls plaque, satisfies the need to chew, and is nutritious. It is highly recommended as a healthy reward for your dog.

one. Most dogs will figure this out very quickly.

Never leave your dog by himself for a long periods of time without his being confined in a safe area. A bored dog will chew.

Another reason dogs chew is because they're anxious. If left alone for long periods of time, many will develop "separation anxiety." This can be caused by a change in their environment such as a recent move, new person or animal in the house, or someone in the family returning to work after having been home for several months.

Separation anxiety causes the most severe destructive tendencies in your dog, especially if he is left loose in the house. Prevent it by keeping him in his crate when you are not home. It also helps to not get into saying long gooey goodbyes, leaving Shadow even more anxious. If you give him a treat as you put him into his enclosure he will not identify your leaving with anything negative. This will maintain your positive

relationship and keep your home intact.

DIGGING

Dogs dig for several reasons. Foremost, it's fun. This isn't much different than human children digging in a sandbox, except that a dog can destroy your yard because he won't confine his play to the sandbox.

Dogs also dig out of boredom, if they catch an interesting scent or if they are hot. Leaving Shadow outside for long periods of time will contribute to turning your beautiful yard into a lunar landscape. Bushes will be dug up and dragged around, holes will appear near the foundation, and fences will get new openings from underneath.

If you don't want to give up your yard for the dog, then you will need to either go outside with him and correct him every time he digs or not leave him outside for a long period of time, especially during the warm months.

To teach your dog not to dig do the following:

Go outside with him and hang onto the end of his leash.

When he begins to dig, tug back on the leash and say "No!" in a low growly tone.

When he stops and goes onto another activity, praise

The Galileo® is the toughest nylon bone ever made. It is flavored to appeal to your dog and has a relatively soft outer layer. It is a wonderful chew toy and doggy pacifier.

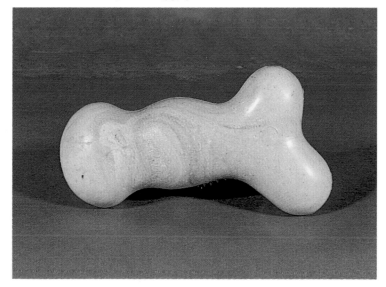

him in a high tone.

If holes are already there, place some of his feces in each hole before you fill it in. Dogs rarely dig up their own feces.

MOUTHING

All puppies will mouth. This behavior is similar to the oral stage that human babies experience. Everything goes into the mouth to taste and explore. An older dog doing this is no longer in an oral phase, but is exhibiting dominance. He will put his mouth on you telling you to play, or relating his dislike for something.

Prevent this from becoming a dangerous situation. Begin by immediately teaching Shadow that mouthing will not be tolerated. If you have a leash on him, simply jerk it quickly as you say No! each time he puts his mouth on you, regardless if he bites down or not. If you don't have a leash on him do the following:

Anytime he puts his mouth on you, grab him by the scruff and look him directly in his eyes.

Say No! in a low growly tone.

When he looks away, let go. As with all the behavior problems, prevention is the best cure. Be consistent in every situation, and Shadow will quickly understand his limitations.

DROP-IT

Many dogs will grab something they know they shouldn't have simply to get you involved in a game of chase. They have learned that if they take something you will want to get it back, and the game begins. Shadow remains still until you get close, then he jumps away or runs a short distance waiting for you to catch up. As soon as you do he takes off again. What fun! At least it is for your dog.

Maybe when you eventually corner him and try to take the object he'll growl at you.

You must never allow an older dog to engage in mouthing. It can become a potentially dangerous show of dominance especially in larger breeds.

Again, this is part of the game. Only the game has changed from chase to tug-of-war. You try to pull the object from his mouth only to tear it, or get his teeth embedded into your hand.

There is an easier way! Teach Shadow to drop it. Begin by keeping him on a leash at all times. As soon as he grabs something he is not supposed to have, grab the leash and bring him to you. Tell him to come and sit if he knows how to do these commands.

Place one hand over the top of his muzzle and the other on the object. Do not pull on the object, only touch it.

As you say drop it squeeze Shadow's lips into his teeth. He will not want to bite himself so he will open his mouth.

When his mouth opens, take the object and release his muzzle. Be certain to praise him when the object falls into your hand.

Some dogs are very possessive, especially when they have procured a forbidden object or favorite toy. You can't let your dog intimidate you under any circumstances. Maintain a firm grip over his muzzle as well as on his collar or leash. Slowly release your hold once the object is out of his mouth. If he continues to growl or snap I recommend you consult a professional trainer.

PUSHINESS AND BEGGING

How many times have you given in to those big brown eyes that watch you while you eat or relax? Does your dog take food from the children, even off their plates?

This is not only a nuisance it's unhealthy for your dog.

Many dogs have sensitive stomachs and can become sick from ingesting unfamiliar foods. Other dogs will become overweight or stop eating their own food.

You should at no time give in to your dog when he wants something. All choices should be yours alone. You decide when he eats, plays and works. You have full control over his diet and exercise. I'm sure some of us have wished

Although begging at the dinner table may seem cute during puppyhood, once your dog is grown, this behavior may lead to serious problems.

If a dog seems to bark for no reason, he is most likely bored. Supply your dog with different toys and activities throughout the day.

squirrels and butterflies, or he is lonely or he just wants to play.

If he is barking because he wants to play, then this is the easiest to cure. The other reasons may be more difficult because you are either not at home or he is loose in the yard and will run from you when you go out to reprimand him, which leaves you screaming at him from the window or doorway, adding to the problem.

As with the other behavior problems, the best cure is to keep Shadow on a leash at all times, inside as well as out. Whenever he barks at nothing (keep in mind that you do want him to bark when someone comes to your home), do the following: bring Shadow to you. Wrap your hand around his muzzle and look directly into his eyes. Say "NO BARK" in a low tone of voice. Slowly release Shadow. Repeat the exercise every time he opens his mouth without reason.

If Shadow is barking when

you are not home you will need to set him up by pretending to leave and returning to

reprimand him every time he barks. It may take a weekend to accomplish this. Be certain to go through the exact routine that you perform every day before leaving for work. Dogs are magnificent body language and routine translators. They'll know if anything is different from normal and will adjust to it accordingly. In some cases you may even need to take your car around the block and sneak back.

If all else fails there are products on the market that can help. There are collars that will either produce a sound, discharge a noxious odor, vibrate or release an electrical stimulant each time the dog barks. Some collars will respond on one bark while others wait until three.

It is as important for our animal friends to have healthy teeth and gums as it is for us. Fortunately, maintaining your dog's oral care is getting easier and easier for the pet owner. Now there's a taste-free, easy-to-use gel that will keep pets' teeth clean, reduce tartar build up and eliminate breath odor. Photo courtesy of Breath Friend™/ American Media Group.

The Basic Commands

Your dog should welcome obedience training. It will lend him an outlet for his energy as well as give him something to focus on. The first step to beginning successful training is familiarizing your dog with his collar and lead.

If you love your dog, then the best present you could ever give him is obedience training. All dogs were bred for a purpose. They have an innate desire to perform their functions and to learn discipline. Obedience training gives them the outlet they are searching for. With new jobs they become focused and happy.

Contrary to popular myth you will not ruin your dog's personality, but instead enhance it. He will become brighter.eyed, more accepting of new situations, and best of all, learn to communicate with you just by learning the basic commands.

HOW TO COMMUNICATE WITH YOUR DOG

Dogs utilize body language, vocal tones, scent, touch and taste in all of their communication with each other. When training a dog it is best to try to emulate the canine language in order to achieve faster success with complete understanding.

When using your voice, keep the frequency to a normal conversational level. A dog hears far better than we do, so there is no reason to shout at any time. Shouting will not get the point across faster, it will only show your dog that you are not in control.

There are three tones of voice you should use when training your dog: a high enthusiastic tone when praising; a demanding authoritative tone preceded by your dog's name when giving a command; and a low growly tone when giving a reprimand.

When praising your dog use the word good repeatedly. When giving a command do so only once, so that your dog will learn to listen on the first command and not wait until you've said it five times. Use the word no with all reprimands.

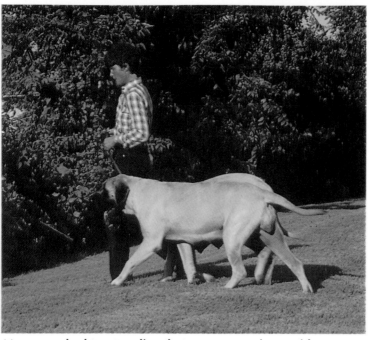

Many people do not realize that we communicate with our pets through more than just our voices. Body language, scent, touch, and taste all play a role in communication.

when he is working and when he is allowed to do his own thing. The word break or finished can be used when releasing him. Don't use the word okay because we all have a tendency to overuse that word, which can confuse your dog if he hears it while working and you didn't mean to release him.

Since dogs also communicate largely with touch, it is best to keep your hands off him while he is working, otherwise he'll be very distracted. Shadow will learn the difference between work and break time faster if he isn't touched while working and is petted when told to break. The exception to this rule however is after he has come to you. At this time he should receive a pat on the head to encourage his good behavior.

Scent is very important when dogs are interacting and can also play a large part in your relationship with Shadow. However, unlike canines we have a difficult

It is important to use these words consistently so that Shadow learns what you are saying. It will take him longer to learn that he is doing something wrong if you use several words such as off, stop it, no, don't, or get down. Simply say "No!" Granted the tone of your voice will clue him in somewhat, but the goal is to teach him the language.

There are several body positions that will be helpful while training. As previously mentioned, dogs communicate with body language. Every movement of the ears, eyes, tail, legs and nose has a meaning in the dog kingdom. When giving a command or a reprimand try to look dominant by standing upright. When greeting your dog, teaching him to come to you, or releasing him from work, crouch down to his level

so that you are on more equal terms.

Everyone needs to hear the bell for quitting time. Your dog isn't any different. You need to communicate to him

The POPpup™ is a healthy treat for your dog. It can be served in bone hard form or microwaved to become a rich cracker, which your dog will love. POPpups™ are available in liver and other flavors and are fortified with calcium.

Your behavior will greatly influence the effectiveness of your training sessions with your dog. Never train when you are frustrated or tired; your dog needs a calm and supportive environment in which to learn.

time sensing emotions and intentions in this manner so we can't utilize it during training.

Food can play a large part in the training process, especially with a very shy dog or one that requires incentive. Very few dogs will turn down a tidbit and many will do almost anything to get it. Food will be utilized more in the training of tricks than in obedience work, however. During obedience work we are teaching Shadow to listen to you, not to the treats.

TEACHING THE HEEL

The more willful your dog, the firmer your training method should be. If your dog is very submissive or fearful, however, begin his training as if he were a young puppy.

Teaching the Heel

For this, you will need a choke chain and a six-foot leather leash. Before putting on the choke chain, measure Shadow's head. Using a tape measure, hold the end on the crown of his head, pass it under his jaw and around to the top again. You will need to add two inches to the measurement for a proper fitting. Make certain that the brand of collar you use is lightweight and has large rounded links. The smaller the links, the harsher the chain.

When putting the training collar together, slip one end of the chain through a ring and slide it through. The rings are the same size so one will fit through the other! Before you put the collar on your dog, present it directly in front of his face in the shape of a P. The loose end will be hanging down and is to be attached to the leash.

To lessen any struggle, put your hand through the collar and hold Shadow's nose as you slide the collar over his head. Once the training collar is on, take off his other collar so that it doesn't interfere with the action of the choke chain. Attach your six-foot leather lead and you're ready to begin.

Hold the loop of the leash in your right hand, along with any extra lead. Place your left hand palm down two feet from Shadow's collar. The leash should dangle down to your dog's shoulder.

1. Take a step forward on your left leg as to say "Shadow, Heel!" in a firm, authoritative tone of voice. If Shadow follows willingly continue walking for 10 to 20 steps. If not, then coax him to you by slapping your left leg.

2. When Shadow is walking with you for up to 20 steps, begin doing turns. This is especially important for those dogs that run ahead or dodge in front of you as you walk. When you turn, jerk on the leash from your shoulder with a straight arm and say "No!" Your turns should be fast and sharp.

3. When Shadow is walking with you, while his eyes are watching you, stop, crouch down and say "Break!" (his release word). Pet him for a minute and begin again.

4. Shadow should now have a vague idea of what you are trying to teach him. As long as he remains at your side, praise him enthusiastically. Whenever he strays from the proper heel position, do a turn and say no. Within a short time he'll remain at your side, attentive to your ever-changing direction.

In order to avoid struggle when first placing the choke collar on your dog, allow him to inspect it and then hold his nose while sliding the collar over his head.

Once a dog understands the heel command it will make walking him in public places a much more pleasurable experience. Your dog will stay close to your side instead of straining to engage everyone you pass.

5. As you work with Shadow, try walking in a square or triangle. This helps you to maintain a direction without starting to follow Shadow to his favorite sniffing spot.

6. Stop often as you say break, then crouch down to pet him. Allow Shadow time to sniff or relieve himself during his rest period. This is his time to lead you around, provided he doesn't lunge. If he does so, tug back on your leash and say "No!"

At no time should your leash be tight. The two rings should be together at all times, except for when you give a smart jerk on the leash.

Teaching the Heel to a Submissive Dog

When working with a submissive dog the best means of keeping his attention, as well as accomplishing training goals, is through bait training. This method makes him both enjoy and look forward to the work. A dog trained with food will learn quickly and have a longer attention span. Food will be far more efficient due to its speedy reinforcement. If you use food, make certain the treats are soft and easy to break. Tear the food into very small pieces so as not to fill Shadow's tummy. Get Shadow's attention by putting a piece of food under his nose. Place yourself on his right side, keeping the food under his nose. Say "Shadow, heel" as you take one step forward with your left leg. When Shadow catches up to you, praise and give him the treat when he catches up. The next time take two steps. Again praise and give him the treat when he catches up. Within minutes you will be able to increase your steps from two to ten before having to reinforce with food.

When you can do 10 steps

without losing Shadow's interest, incorporate a turn into your steps. The easiest turn will be to the right. Keep the food under Shadow's nose as you change directions and stop shortly after the turn.

By the end of your 15 minute session, Shadow should be able to walk with you short distances and do several turns before stopping and eating his treat.

If Shadow gets distracted at any time, stop walking and put the food directly under his nose. When he reaches for the food, draw him back to your leg. If he is repeatedly distracted, take him to a quieter area or a hard surface with fewer odors.

Shadow will learn best with short, frequent training sessions. Don't try to work with your dog after 15 minutes, especially if he is repeatedly losing interest. A short training session two or three times per day is far more effective than a half-hour once a day.

TEACHING THE SIT

Begin teaching the sit by

first working Shadow at the heel. After the first five minutes of this training session he should be settled enough to learn the new behavior.

It is important to begin your training in a quiet, secluded area where neither you nor your dog will be disturbed.

Before stopping, gather your leash by sliding it through your left hand, and when your left hand touches the stitching or braiding of the leash, place

it against your left thigh and immediately stop walking.

As soon as you stop, tell Shadow to sit by saying his name first and then commanding "Sit!" with authority. If your dog sits automatically, then praise him enthusiastically and go directly into the heel. If Shadow just stands at your side or pulls, then transfer the leash into your right hand, keeping the leash against your left thigh. This will free your left hand to place him into the sit.

Using your left forefinger and thumb placed just above his hind leg bones, gently press into the hollow and push down at the same time. As soon as he sits, praise him, loosen the leash and go directly into the heel. Repeat this exercise every 10 to 20 steps.

Every dog is different. While some may learn to sit quickly, others will be stubborn about putting their rears down when they would rather be in motion. Maintain your patience and persistence and don't become frustrated. He will learn to sit provided you remain consistent.

If Shadow begins pulling back or sitting crookedly, it will help to heel and stop along

The sit command will help to keep your dog controlled and disciplined at all times. A well-trained dog will be able to accompany you almost anywhere and participate in all aspects of your life.

he sits at your side, transfer the entire leash into your left hand. Say his name and the command stay! as you bring your right hand in front of his face with the fingers pointed downward and spread. This will present him with a large visual cue for the command. Step in front of him with your right leg. One step should allow you to pivot from the heel position to facing him directly. Keep your leash loose but off the ground so that he doesn't entangle himself if he tries to leave the sit/stay position. If he does get up, say "No!" in your low reprimand tone and replace him in the same spot. Don't move around with him if he tries to sit elsewhere. He should remain where you originally told him to stay.

Once you have returned him to the spot again, say his name and give the stay command. The stay command is repeated due to your dog not being in the exact same position as he was originally, unless you can correct him when he is thinking about moving and he returns himself to the same place, in which case you do not repeat the command.

After having him maintain the stay for only a couple seconds, return to the heel position by pivoting back into place. Hesitate five to ten seconds and go into the heel.

After Shadow remains comfortably for five seconds, gradually increase the amount of time he must stay. This is one of the places successive approximation is used. With each successive stay command make Shadow work harder to complete the criterion for a proper

response. Make certain to praise him throughout the time he is being good. So, if Shadow remains in place without trying to get up and watches you attentively then tell him he's a good dog in a happy tone of voice.

Shadow should not be allowed to sniff when performing the stay or any

other command, nor should he lay down while staying. This is a sit/stay not a down/stay, so it must be made clear that the positions are very different and he is to listen and learn the meanings of the words.

Within several days Shadow should be able to remain in a sit/stay for a full

A well-trained retriever will sit at his master's side obediently throughout all kinds of commotion.

These two Labradors are surely awaiting their next command. During training a dog should be alert and focused at all times.

If Shadow does well with this minimal movement then increase your movement on the next stay to include walking along each of his sides as well as in front of him. Do this for several stay exercises.

When Shadow is comfortable with your moving along both of his sides and is remaining in place relaxed, then try to walk all the way around him. He is more likely to remain in place if you walk around his back end first as you begin the circle.

The next time you do the stay, go around him in both directions. Increase the amount of circles you walk around Shadow with each stay command and remember to change direction often or Shadow will only accept your movement in one direction. Another problem with walking only one way is that you might get very dizzy.

Half way through this training session Shadow will be able to remain in position with you walking around him in both directions. Now it is time for the next step.

Step 3: Distance
Continue to work with the previous step but begin to add a foot in distance during each stay command.

Be certain to continue walking around Shadow as you increase the distance or it will be more noticeable that something is different, in which case Shadow may be more likely to move. Within five stay exercises you should be walking freely around Shadow at the end of the leash. If at any time Shadow breaks his position, say "No!" immediately and return him

minute. He is now ready for the next step.

Step 2: Movement
After practicing for a few minutes with the heel and sit/stay Shadow should be ready to accept a new facet of the stay exercise.

Perform the stay exactly as you have been doing. This time, however, do not just stand still in front of him. Move side-to-side one step in each direction.

The next time you do the stay, move side-to-side two steps in each direction. Be certain to remain close and in front of him at this time.

to the same spot as quickly as you can. Do not allow him to begin heeling before you give the command.

Now that Shadow knows how to heel, sit, and stay it is time to present him with distractions so that he'll learn to listen to you no matter what the situation. The best distractions to begin with are his favorite toys.

Ask someone to throw the toys around you and Shadow as you work. Be certain to instruct your helper not to say your dog's name, give a command, or let the toys land directly next to you.

As you work with this distraction-proofing exercise keep in mind that Shadow is looking to you for leadership and guidance. Therefore, if you are distracted, he too will react to the situation. Concentrate on what you are doing and ignore the actions of your helper or any other natural distractions that may be present.

Shadow will most likely want to go after the toys or your helper, especially if your helper runs around and slaps his legs, which is a great distraction. Firmly and consistently correct your dog.

Give a quick tug in the opposite direction in which he is pulling. The tug should be fast and firm, causing a choke chain to click. You must release the collar as quickly as you tugged it or you'll only end up pulling on Shadow's neck instead of correcting him.

When Shadow can heel and sit/stay with his toys flying through the air and people running alongside him as he works, then he is ready for the ultimate distraction—another dog!

TEACHING THE DOWN/STAY

The down can be the most difficult behavior to teach a dog. Lying down is a submissive position, and your dog will only do it if he has complete respect for you. Therefore it is imperative that your dog be working well on the previous exercises before

The down command may be the most difficult for your dog to accept. In the wild the down represents a submissive stance, once your dog realizes this isn't the case he should catch on quickly.

Once you have given the down command be sure to follow through no matter how difficult it may be to get your dog into position.

teaching this one.

He shouldn't be playing with you while he works, such as jumping up and nipping, grabbing the leash, planting his rear end, or picking up sticks and leaves while walking. If he is doing these things at any point during your training sessions, then work with him until he stops completely. Many dogs will misbehave when they are tired, but it is still not an excuse for allowing Shadow to get away with the problems.

When teaching this exercise it is important not to lose your patience or to become frustrated. Also, if you have given the down command make certain to follow through no matter how difficult it may be to place your dog in position.

You can make the down more positive by petting Shadow on the belly when he lies down, or using food to bait him into position. Another means of making certain that the exercise remains positive is to always praise enthusiastically. Most dogs thrive on praise, so don't skimp!

Another important factor at this point in your training is to vary your exercises. Don't do the same thing over and over or you will be pattern-training versus obedience training. This is especially true when teaching the down. Do not command Shadow to do the down every time you stop. Do it every two or three times. In between, have him stop and sit, or sit and stay, or do a sit/stay and then a down/stay. The more you vary the exercises the more attentive Shadow will become.

Work Shadow in the

When your dog is able to remain in the down for several minutes, begin presenting him with distractions. If he is able to remain in place you can be sure that he will obey no matter what is happening around him.

heeling exercises for five minutes or until he is working well. Upon stopping, have Shadow sit and then transfer your leash into your left hand. Point downwards with your right forefinger directly in front of Shadow's nose as you command "Down!" in a very authoritative tone of voice. Shadow may look at your visual cue, he may even sniff at it. This is a positive reaction. However, very few dogs will follow the cue into the down position. Place your left hand (still holding the leash) onto Shadow's shoulder blades. Bring your right hand underneath his right foreleg and grab his left foreleg. Sweep his forelegs forward as you apply pressure on his shoulder blades.

As soon as he is lying down, give him the stay command by placing your right hand in front of his face with the fingers spread as you say "Stay!" Maintain light pressure on his shoulder blades, and if you feel him trying to get up apply more pressure. Before Shadow has a chance to get up go directly into the heel.

If you feel your dog relaxing into the down position you can release the pressure on his shoulder blades. Remain aware that he may at any time try to get up and you will need to reapply the pressure.

When Shadow is able to remain in the down/stay without any pressure on his shoulders, then gradually increase the time of his stay command. At this time you can begin walking around him as you did during the sit/stay. The only difference is that instead of walking side-to-side in front of him you'll be walking side-to-side along his right side and working your way around him from behind.

Within several training sessions you should be able to walk around Shadow at the end of the leash and also walk over him. Now is also the time to begin presenting distractions again to make certain he performs the down/stay no matter what is going on around him.

hour and he is coming because you brought the car and he wants to go for a ride. Never reprimand Shadow when he comes!

You will be most inviting if you call your dog while in a crouched position with your arms open wide. Your tone of voice should be high-pitched and happy. Chasing Shadow will have the opposite effect—he will run farther and faster,

Either make certain he is in a fenced-in area or keep him on a leash at all times.

The recall command will need to be practiced from all positions and angles, teaching Shadow to come no matter where you are, whether he can see you or not. He should perform the exercise by first turning to look at you, then walking directly to you and, upon reaching you, sit facing

Recall command. When your dog is coming to you from an off lead situation he must pass behind you, take up his position and then sit. This command is very helpful when training a dog for the field or just letting him have a run in the park.

TEACHING THE RECALL (COME)

The recall is one of the most important commands to teach your dog. This command should be the most pleasant thing your dog could perform. Whenever he comes to you always praise him enthusiastically even if you've been chasing him for the past

enjoying the "game."

To prevent this game of tag, always keep your dog on a leash until he is reliable off lead on all commands. He may want to remain close to you when he is insecure, but once he acclimates to a new situation he will become more independent and curious.

you. He should remain in the sit until you tell him otherwise.

By this point in your training Shadow should be able to heel, sit, down, and stay with distractions. It is very important to accomplish these things before attempting the recall, for you cannot control him properly in order to teach this new command if he doesn't stay for at least a minute in any position.

The procedures for this command are the same regardless of the training collar you are using. In fact, the collar will rarely be used while executing the Recall, provided you utilize the proper vocal and visual cues. Remember, the dog must want to come to you.

Now, that's not saying that you will never have to use the leash. There will be times when Shadow would rather go chase a bird or butterfly than come to you directly. Or, there may be someone who just arrived that Shadow absolutely must say hello to. So do not drop your leash under any circumstances and be ready to utilize a quick correction if necessary. Just do not use the leash to drag Shadow to you.

Work with Shadow for five minutes with the exercises he already understands. This

The recall command should be the most pleasant command your dog performs. Coming to you should always result in enthusiasm and praise for your dog.

always allows him to settle into paying attention before you begin new things.

As a general rule, when training, begin with the things that Shadow will easily perform. Then go to the more difficult or newer concepts that he has learned recently.

Your dog will be a happy and content pet once trained. You may even find that a stronger bond has developed between you both because of the time you've spent in training.

When he is performing those well, it is time to learn a totally new behavior.

Place Shadow in a sit/stay and walk around him in both directions. Work your way to the end of the leash as you walk. 3. Stop in front of him and turn to face him. Bend at the waist and say his name and then the command come in a pleasant, welcoming tone of voice.

Shadow will naturally want to come to you because you look welcoming. In fact, it'll be rough to resist. As he comes in, gather your leash so that he doesn't step on it while he approaches. Keep the leash in front of you attached to your middle so that Shadow can come directly to you. Do not allow him to go beyond you and do not move to intercept him.

If he begins to go around you, walk straight backwards two to four steps as you continue to gather the leash. This guides him to "front," which is another term for a proper recall.

If Shadow tries to sniff on his way to you or wants to go say hello to someone else, then give a sharp tug on the leash. When he has returned his attention to you praise him enthusiastically. Always praise Shadow as he comes to you.

When he arrives in front of you, give him the sit command. If he does not sit, then place him. Do not repeat the command or jerk on his collar. Remember this should be completely pleasant! After he sits, give him a light pat on the head as you praise him, then return to heel position and walk forward.

Repeat this exercise from the down/stay position, and call him from in front of him, off to either side, and especially from behind. Shadow should come to you regardless of from where you are calling him. If you only call to him when you are facing him then that is the only situation in which he will execute the command.

Another time that this behavior can be practiced is during Shadow's break time. Every once in a while call him to come and sit when he is involved in other activities, such as playing with another dog or sniffing something interesting. If Shadow doesn't respond within five seconds be certain to give a sharp jerk on the leash as you say "No!" When he begins to respond, praise him enthusiastically.

Keep in mind that whatever visual cue you begin with, you will need to continue using it in order for Shadow to understand your command. If you begin slapping your legs when you want him to come

from his break time, then you will need to continue doing the same at all other times. It can sometimes be difficult to slap one's legs when holding a leash.

I suggest that you use simple body positions along with the vocal command for this will be far easier for the dog to understand and for other family members to emulate. Consistency is the key to reliability!

TEACHING THE STAND

This exercise will come in handy in many situations. Most importantly it teaches your dog to remain still while being examined by you or a veterinarian. Shadow will also come to understand what is happening to him and will become less stressed when confronted with this circumstance. Best of all, your veterinarian will love seeing you.

Teaching the stand command will pay off in many practical, everyday situations, such as trips to the veterinarian and groomer.

The stand will allow your dog to remain still during sometimes stressful situations. This new calm will help your dog better understand what is going on around him.

The stand is also a great way to teach your dog to remain still while being groomed and checked for parasites. It can be annoying when Shadow wants to bite at the brush or moves around just when you thought you saw a little black insect in his dense fur coat. If he remained still during these procedures, not only would Shadow receive a more thorough brushing and check-over, but both of you would enjoy the experience. When something is enjoyable it is done more often.

There are two parts to teaching your dog to stand. The first is getting him to remain still at your side while you hold him, and the second is to teach him to remain in one place while you walk

A healthy treat for your dog, CHOOZ® are made of cheese, are low in fat, and are 70% protein. Your dog can eat his CHOOZ® in bone hard form or microwaved to a biscuit like consistency.

around him. He can move his head around to watch you and wag his tail as you praise him, but his feet should remain in one spot.

You can have your dog go into the stand from any position, but the easiest way is from a sit. If you try doing this exercise from a down you'll have to lift Shadow, and if he weighs 150 pounds you may end up in traction.

Work Shadow through his heeling exercises until he is paying attention most of the time. After he sits at your side place all of the leash in your right hand. Place your left hand with the fingers spread and palm facing your dog near his head. Say "Shadow, stand." Move your left hand down to Shadow's solar plexus (just below the rib cage). Pull forward, not up, on the leash. This will get Shadow's weight off his haunches. Lift under Shadow's tummy simultaneously as you pull forward.

As soon as Shadow is standing begin rubbing his tummy gently, release the pull of the leash and put a few fingers of your right hand through his collar to keep his front end from going anywhere. Go directly into the heel exercise. Shadow will love the Stand. He'll be getting petted and praised throughout. If Shadow tries to move, say "No," and replace him in the same spot. Do not pull on the leash to correct him.

Repeat this exercise at least 10 times during your training sessions. Make certain to mix it into the other behaviors so that Shadow doesn't get the idea that he is supposed to stand when you stop instead of sit.

Once in the standing position be sure that your dog is placing his weight evenly on all four feet. He must stand squarely with his forelegs and hindlegs parallel.

It is far easier to groom a dog that will sit and stand as needed. Grooming a well-trained dog will be an enjoyable experience for you both.

When Shadow can maintain the standing position for up to 30 seconds, you can begin teaching him to stay as you walk around him.

After placing him in the stand make certain that he is placing his weight evenly on all four feet. To do so he must stand squarely with his forelegs and hind legs parallel.

Keep your left hand on Shadow's tummy and continue to rub. He'll most likely remain in place if he's enjoying himself. Place the leash between your knees and give the stay signal with your right hand as you say "Shadow, stay." Take your leash back into your right hand and begin to walk around Shadow, his back end first. Remember, keep rubbing his tummy! Don't go all the way around him on

There is only one acceptable material for flossing human teeth and that's nylon. Nylafloss® allows your dog to chew on real nylon. It will also encourage interaction with your dog through tug-o-war games, in which you will be slowly pulling the nylon strands through your dog's teeth.

this first try. Only venture to his other side and then return around his back end to heel position. Once back, go directly into the heel.

As Shadow learns to remain still you can go completely around him and begin to rub his back, head, ears and lift his tail. All these physical manipulations prepare him for a trip to the veterinarian, groomer or the bath tub.

It's far easier to bathe a dog who will lie down to get soaked, stand to get shampooed, and lie down again to get rinsed. You might actually make it out of the dog washing without looking as if you bathed with him!

The Spinach Bone™ by Nylabone is 100% edible and enhanced with dog-friendly ingredients. They contain no salt, sugar, alcohol, plastic, or perservatives.

Game Time!

and trick work. The main distinction is that with obedience work you are making your dog do what you command. With trick work you are encouraging Shadow to work, using food and coercion to increase his excitement. Although the tricks may be more fun, the control of proper obedience training is a requirement for optimum results.

There are some tricks that will help Shadow occupy his time, thereby giving him something to do when you are busy. Many of the tricks may be helpful if you decide to further pursue advanced obedience training, tracking or other dog-related activities.

It is best to make certain that Shadow fully understands his obedience training before you try to teach the tricks, otherwise he may become confused or overly excited. He needs to know the basic sit, down and stay to perform the shake, roll-over and flip-the-treat.

Each trick must be taught by breaking down the goal into smaller parts. This is called successive approximation. We used this when teaching the stay command. On each successive command we required Shadow to perform more. He began by sitting still for a short amount of time and worked toward your walking around him at the end of the leash.

Once your dog is well-trained in basic obedience commands you may want to teach him some tricks. Not only will your dog enjoy the new experiences, but it will also be a lot of fun for you.

Many dogs enjoy learning how to perform tricks. Not only is this a great means of teaching him new things, it's also a lot of fun. You will also be the hit at any party as you and your dog provide the entertainment.

There is a big difference between obedience training

SHAKE

This is the easiest trick for Shadow because he already

Shake is the easiest trick you can teach your dog.

does this naturally when he wants your attention. How many times have you been sitting watching your favorite television show and gotten a leg propped upon yours?

This behavior can be channeled to be performed upon command instead of on whim. Make certain that Shadow doesn't mistake the teaching of this command to mean that he can return to pawing you for attention.

Place Shadow in a Sit/Stay. Stand in front of him, holding a treat in your left hand. You should draw his attention toward that hand, turning his head slightly, which will shift his weight to that side. As you say "shake" lift his left paw with your right hand while you simultaneously give him the treat with your left hand.

When his paw rests in your right hand, hold it briefly and praise him.

Repeat the former steps but this time don't lift his paw, only touch it from underneath

so that he lifts it himself. When he does so, give him the treat and praise him.

When he is readily lifting his leg, go to touching it on the front. He gets his treat when he lifts his paw and you are holding it in your hand.

Now, only hold out your right hand without touching his left leg as you present the treat and say "shake." If he

doesn't do the behavior within 10 seconds, back-track to the previous step. If he does perform properly, give him his treat and praise. He now knows how to shake!

ROLL OVER

Any dog who has learned how to lie down on command can easily perform this classic trick. The first step is to teach

When teaching your dog a new trick using food treats, he will respond more readily. Before you know it he will be the life of the party.

All dogs like to feel appreciated. Once your dog knows how to perform even the simplest of tricks, he will revel in the attention he gets and the excitement he creates when performing them.

Shadow to lie in a very relaxed manner, similar to playing dead but without his feet in the air. He will tend to roll in the opposite direction of where his legs are stretched. While it is easiest for him to go in this direction, he can be taught to go either way with a simple shift of his hips.

Place Shadow in a down. Stand in front of him and put a treat directly near his nose. When he cues in on the food, bring it around toward the back of his head so that his nose is facing his back. When he follows the food, give the roll over command and help him over by bringing his back legs around in the same direction as his nose. This will help him roll completely over.

When you give the visual cue of making a circle with your finger, make certain the direction of the cue coincides with the direction Shadow is

Once your dog is able to perform the down command, teaching him to roll over will be simple. Begin by teaching your dog to lay down in a very relaxed manner.

rolling. Otherwise both of you may become confused.

When Shadow has completed the roll, praise him, give him the treat and

coax him into a sit or standing position.

Each time you repeat the exercise you can gradually reduce the physical help as

"Splendor in the grass." It seems that this Mastiff has taken his roll over training to heart.

Before attempting to teach your dog to sit up be sure he is free of all hip and back problems or the trick could cause him discomfort.

well as the movements of your hand. Eventually all you'll need to do is make a circle with your finger and Shadow will roll over.

SIT UP

Before attempting this trick make certain that your dog doesn't have any hip or elbow problems that can cause discomfort when placing all his weight onto his hind quarters.

It will help your dog to teach this exercise in a corner where he can feel secure against the wall and reduce any chance of flipping over backwards, which can cause him to dislike the exercise.

To begin this trick Shadow must first be able to sit squarely. That means his weight should be evenly distributed on both haunches without leaning one way or the other. This will afford him better balance, allowing him to lift his forelegs off the floor. If you are outside you can offer him a back rest by standing behind him.

Place him in a sit/stay. Hold a treat just over his nose so that he can see and smell it but not reach it. Say "Up" as you draw his attention ever

higher. Go slowly and make certain that his body follows his nose upward. If not, allow him to put a paw on you for support.

As soon as Shadow shows the effort of lifting his front legs, give him the treat. Gradually increase the criterion with each successful exercise until he is sitting up over his haunches without using any support.

When Shadow performs this trick readily you can begin to gain distance from him when you give the up command. This is done similarly to the elongation of the stay command. You first build up the time, then movement, and finally distance.

FLIP THE TREAT

Although this trick looks really complicated it is actually a simple extension of the sit/stay with distractions. It will take time,

When first learning how to sit up, your dog may be more comfortable in a corner where he cannot fall, or putting a paw on you to steady himself.

however, for Shadow to learn to catch an object on the fly. It will help if you use the same sized treats at all times during this exercise.

Place Shadow in a sit/stay. Stand in front of Shadow and place a treat on his nose. Hold his nose steady as you place the treat. If he tries to get up at any time, tell him no and replace him in the same spot. Be certain to remain calm and do all your movements gently. This will transfer over to Shadow and keep him from getting hyper about having the treat so close that he can taste it.

There are all kinds of flying disks for dogs and kids, but only one brand is made just for dogs with strength and originality. The Nylabone® Frisbee™ is a must if you want to have this sort of fun with your dog. Don't use cheap imitation, plastic flying disks. Look for the name Nylabone® Frisbee™ to be sure it's specially made for dogs. The trademark Frisbee is used under license from Mattel, Inc., California, USA.

Flipping the treat may take a little work, but your dog will do just about anything to get to that tasty morsel you place on his nose.

Since we used the word break to release Shadow from his other exercises, we will utilize the same verbal cue to allow Shadow to leave the strenuous sit/stay and get that treat! As soon as you give the release word, Shadow will snap his head to get the treat.

Even if the food goes flying across the room, allow him to break his stay to retrieve it. It takes time to learn to keep it close enough to reach the mouth before falling. You may need to experiment with the placement on his nose to see which position is easiest for him. Most dogs do well if the treat is placed just behind the nostrils where the bare skin turns into fur.

FIND A TOY

There are actually two parts to this trick. The first is to get Shadow to cue in on the scent of the toy by using food to entice him—unless he's so crazy about the toy that he'll want it no matter what, in which case you can pass over the first procedure.

Begin by allowing your dog to have a treat. The next time, you present the food to him in a sit/stay and allow him to smell it but not to eat it. If he tries to take the food tell him no and move it away from him. Be certain you move it quickly or your fingers might end up as part of his snack.

Again present the treat without letting him have it. When you see his nostrils move, praise him and move the food a few feet away and place it on the floor. Now tell him "break, find it!" Allow him to go for the food. When Shadow reaches the food praise him enthusiastically. He's going to like this game.

Not only does he get treats but also praise for eating them!

Each time you repeat this trick place the food further and further away. Allow him to watch you carry it and place it so that he will always be successful in finding it.

When he can find the food in another room (in plain sight), it is time to hide the treat. Although you are putting the food in another room, place it somewhere that he can't miss it as soon as he enters the room.

Gradually make the game more difficult by hiding the treat behind furniture, on the bottom tier of a bookshelf, a stair, or eventually under a throw rug. The more difficult the game, the more enjoyment for you and your dog.

If Shadow begins having trouble locating the food, then back up a few steps and proceed from there. Although you may be tempted to rush into utilizing difficult hiding places, you must slow down and allow Shadow to progress at his own pace. This is especially important when working with an older dog who has never been involved in this type of training.

When Shadow is adept at locating a treat, you can transfer the game into finding a toy. You must use his favorite toy for this to work. It also helps if he is a natural retriever. If not, you may want to either follow him to the hiding place and give him his reward and praise at that time, or leave a treat next to the toy so that when Shadow finds it he'll receive an immediate reward.

There are specific breeds of dogs that do better at certain tricks than others. This is not to say that if your dog is not of this breed that he can't perform the trick. It may just take a little more determination on your part.

Sporting breeds, such as retrievers and spaniels, will

Although you can teach your dog just about anything, some breeds will find certain tasks easier to perform than others will.

Remember that there are many tricks your dog is capable of. During a simple game of catch your dog will amaze you with his ability to never miss a throw.